Rumpelstiltskin

Sticker Activity Book

Nick and Claire Page

Illustrations by Sara Baker

How to use this book
Pull out the sticker sheets and have them by you when
you look at each page.

•

Read the story and use the stickers on sheet 1
to fill in the missing pictures and words.
The blue shapes are for "people" or "things" (nouns)
and the yellow shapes are for key words.

•

Look at the stickers on sheet 2 and find the items
that have been removed from the sticker picture.
Now use some of the extra stickers to complete the picture.

•

Have fun making silly sentences using the color-coded
stickers on sheet 3.

•

Mix and match the stickers of heads, bodies, and feet
on sheet 4 to create crazy characters.
Give them names and invent a story about them!

•

Always check that the sticker you have chosen will
fit before you put it in place.

make
believe
ideas

There once was a  miller, who spun a tale to a king. "My daughter can turn straw into gold using a spinning wheel," he said. The king locked the girl in a room full of straw. "Turn all this straw into gold or you will die," he said. The girl burst into tears.

A magic  trapdoor appeared, and out came a little man. "I can spin straw into gold," he said. "But in return, you must give me your first baby." The girl thought. "If I don't, I will die anyway." So she agreed. The little man turned all the straw into gold.

Then he left through the magic  trapdoor. The king was pleased when he saw the gold. He married the girl and she became his queen. The next year she had a baby. One evening, she was looking after the baby when the magic trapdoor appeared and out popped the little  man. "Give me the baby!" he said. "No! Take me!" cried the queen. "I will return in three days," the little man said. "If you guess my name, you can keep the baby. But if not, he is mine. Then he left through the magic trapdoor.

The  queen sent her servants to find out his name, but no one could discover it . On the third day, a messenger arrived. " In the faraway mountains," he said, " I saw a little man dancing and shouting: 'Soon I will have the baby. I'm a clever Rumpelstiltskin!'"

That [evening], the little [man] appeared again. "Can [you] guess my name?" he asked. The [queen] paused. "Is it RUMPELSTILTSKIN?" she asked. The little [man] said, "Noooooooo!" He got so angry that BANG! he burst like a [balloon]. And he [and] his magic [trapdoor] were never seen again.

Sticker picture

Use the stickers on sheet 2 to complete this picture. First find stickers for the missing items and put them in place. Then use some of the extra stickers to add to the picture and make it your own.

Silly sentences

Have fun making silly sentences using the color-coded stickers on sheet 3. The green stickers are "doing" words (verbs). The red stickers are "describing" words (adjectives). The blue stickers are for "people" or "things" (nouns).

Who (cooked) the (wobbly) (🧍) ?

The girl ⬭ the ⬭ ⬭ .

The wicked ⬭ tickled the ⬭ ⬭ .

Rumpelstiltskin ⬭ the ⬭ ⬭ .

The 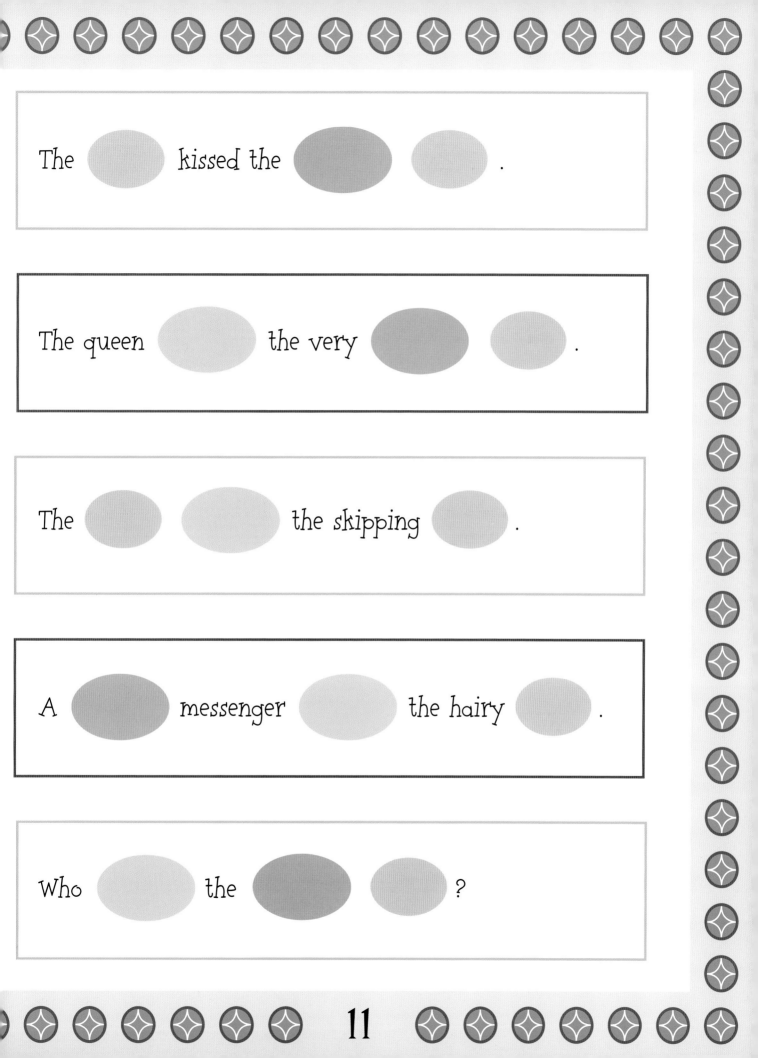 kissed the .

The queen the very .

The the skipping .

A messenger the hairy .

Who the ?

Silly people

Mix and match the stickers on sheet 4 to create some silly people.
Give them names and invent a story about them!